The Reluctant Project Manager

Jeffrey Probst, PMP

The Reluctant Project Manager
Copyright © 2017 by Jeffrey L. Probst

Published by Outland Publishing.
Assisted by CreateSpace, an Amazon company.

Email: outlandpub@yahoo.com

Dedicated to those managers in my career who forced me into the role of project manager. Because of them, I grew and found a new career path.

Introduction

You are good at what you do. In fact you are so good, management has decided you should lead a new project in your area of responsibility. Perhaps even you believe you should be the one to guide the project, after all, you are excellent at what you do. But then you realize project management is not what you want to be doing with your career, or you are not a born leader. Congratulations, you are about to become a reluctant project manager.

Not everyone is suited to be a project manager, nor do they desire to be one. However, sometimes good technical employees are put in charge of a project, even though they lack leadership skills and project management training. This is management's mistake, not yours. You should feel great that management trusts you enough to lead a project, but the last thing anyone wants is for you to fail. That's where this book comes into play.

Unless you desire to be a fulltime project manager, you don't need to learn all about project management. As with most things, 20% of the knowledge is used 80% of the time. To succeed, you need only learn and use that vital 20% of project management. Though small, this book is mighty. Follow its advice and wisdom, and you will have a successful project.

You are good at what you do, and you can be a good project manager too, albeit a reluctant one.

Table of Contents

1 - Project People   7

2 - The Kickoff   11

3 – Communicate   13

4 - Triple Constraint   17

5 - The Schedule   19

6 - Execute the Plan   23

7 – Celebrate   27

8 - Not-Too-Soft Skills   29

Author   34

1

Project People

Identifying all the people affected by the project is the first key to your success. Likely, there are more than anyone first thinks. There are three types of people that care about projects: Decision makers, Consulters, and Informed. Memorizing "DCI" may help you remember these types, which is helpful when placing people in one of the following four groups.

Sponsor
Usually, there is only one sponsor. He/she is a high ranking executive whose area of responsibility most benefits by the project. He must be high enough up the ladder to request resources from other executives, whether or not they are within his area of command.

Depending on the company and nature of the project, the project may be funded by the sponsor's budget. This gives him the right to make key decisions about the project scope, schedule, and cost. The sponsor endorses and defends the project, helping others see it as a valuable investment.

Professional project managers insist on naming a sponsor before a project starts. You would be wise to do the same, since the success of the project team often depends on a sponsor who is willing to step up to the plate when tough decisions must be made. The sponsor also gives authority to the project manager to manage the resources assigned to the project.

Sponsors are not typically on the project team. But that doesn't mean they lack decision making authority, or shouldn't be consulted at times.

Project Manager

There is one, and only one project manager. This ensures the project will receive direction from a unified source, and one person is ultimately responsible for seeing everything gets done.

As a project manager, people sometimes asked me what I did. My response was, "I don't *do* anything. I get everyone else to do it." While this is not entirely true, it gets across an important point. The project manager leads the team. The project team does most of the work.

The project manager still has plenty to do, though. He directs all of the team meetings and planning, documents those plans, holds the team accountable, controls the scope and costs, and informs stakeholders of the project status.

Throughout the duration of the project, it is important to appear calm and in control. Everyone is looking to the project manager for direction, information, and assurance.

Project Team

Keep the project team small. Allow one team member per affected department. Each team member represents and leads the efforts of their department, and are project leaders for their department. They do not assume any of the roles of the project manager, but should direct the actual work within their department, then report back to the project manager.

To determine who may best represent a department on a project team, think back to the DCI acronym. A person with decision-making authority is best. If that is not feasible, then use someone with consultant abilities. The reason for having a decision maker is to expedite the project. It can slow the process when a team member has to go back to their department for key decisions.

Stakeholders

Projects typically have many stakeholders throughout a company. Basically, anyone who has an interest in a project is a stakeholder, including of course, the project team. It is the project manager's duty to identify all stakeholders for the project. This can be quickly done by talking with each department manager. Be aware some projects may have stakeholders outside the company.

The project manager should send out a project status report to all stakeholders on a regular basis. Weekly is a commonly recommended frequency. Status can change quickly. By providing a weekly status report, no one gets surprised too late.

2

The Kickoff

Project kickoffs come in two forms. One is where every possible stakeholder is invited, and the other is where only the project team is invited. I *strongly* recommend the latter.

The only time to include all possible stakeholders is when a major project is being introduced to a company, and the stakeholders and team members are not known yet. Then the sponsor should lead the kickoff meeting, and should hand over the reins to the project manager towards the end of the meeting. Identify all stakeholders and a project team. This might be a good opportunity for the project manager to explain why only one person from each department should be on the project team.

A better kickoff is when only the project team is invited. Plan for a one hour meeting, and never more than two hours. The project manager explains how the project will be managed, and each team member's responsibilities. If the project manager's authority is in question, then invite the project sponsor to clarify the issue.

Discuss the role of each team member. Reiterate how they are responsible for the work done within their department, and how they will communicate progress back to the project manager.

The project manager has the authority to work with department managers to obtain resources for the project. Should an assigned resource be pulled from the project, even temporarily, the project manager must be notified. He can determine the possible affects to the project, and negotiate with the department manager, if needed.

During the kickoff meeting, the scope of the project may or may not be known. If it is, then hand out the scope documents, and discuss it briefly. If not, then identify who will provide the scope. Without knowing what the project must produce, it is impossible to create a plan or a schedule.

The project manager will discuss with the team how they will communicate amongst the team. Involve team members in all discussions. They need to feel they are an important part of the project, because they are. Let them know they will provide due dates for their department's work, and that you (the project manager) will hold them to their agreed schedule.

Create a culture for the project team. Not only will they be held accountable to meet the schedule, but they must strive to *do things right the first time*. There won't be time for costly rework. Do not plan on overtime. Save it for emergencies.

It is unlikely a touchdown will be scored on any kickoff, much less a kickoff meeting. But at least the project will be underway. Feel darn lucky if you're on the twenty-yard line.

3

Communicate

Projects can fail. Lack of, or improper communication is most often to blame. I have occasionally been accused of over-communicating, to which I reply, "Thank you. How nice of you to notice."

Never be afraid of too much communication. Be very afraid of too little. Here, I'll talk about your two best communication tools—team meetings and status reporting.

There are many channels of communications on a project. That is one of the reasons to keep a project team small. A communication channel exists between each and every team member. For each additional team member, another communication channel is added for every member. Large teams are subject to chaotic team meetings.

Regular team meetings are a great forum for communicating among the team. Start on time, and if anyone is late, tell them so. They will soon learn to be on time, at least to your meetings. Give each person a chance to speak, and encourage them to do so. They can report how their progress is going, discuss any issues, or ask questions.

The project manager may remind each team member of their commitments, then ask if they are on track. Beware of the word "try." When someone says, "I'll try to do it," it usually means they *won't*. Get a commitment they will do it. Yoda was right—there is no try, only do.

If anyone is behind schedule, discuss with the team how the task can get back on track. It is imperative team members know they will be held accountable to the team, and the project's success will reflect on all team members.

Project status reporting is the sole responsibility of the project manager. Weekly reporting is usually sufficient, but short projects may demand more frequent reports. Send the status report to all stakeholders. Email works great for distribution, but always attach the status report for easy printing.

What does a good status report contain? Provide an executive summary at the top, followed by details. Then whoever just wants a quick status can easily get it. Those who like to dive into the weeds can read it all.

The executive summary should contain:
- Project name
- Project manager's name
- Current phase(s)
- Phase status (ahead, on track, behind, in trouble)
- Phase % complete
- Phase estimated completion date

The body of the status report may have sections for:
- Outstanding Issues
- Recent accomplishments
- Action items
- Current risks

Provide an executive summary line for each uncompleted phase of the project, even if it has not been started.

Each outstanding issue, recent accomplishment, and action item should include a description, the assignee, and an estimated completion date.

Current risks should include a description and the owner of each risk. List only risks that are currently pertinent for the project. Risks are things that *may* affect the project. Once it actually does affect the project, then it becomes an issue. While risks can be positive or negative, positive risks are rare and can be excluded from the status report.

There is great power in delivering meaningful status reports. Not only is everyone kept informed, the team realizes the importance and visibility of their work. As for the project manager, the status report reflects heavily on his perceived ability. It is a small part of his work, but it is the only part some stakeholders ever see.

There are many forms of communication. Some are more effective than others—much more. Following are five types of communication. Each has their place, but using the inappropriate type for the wrong occasion can be disastrous.

- One-on-one meetings should be used for confidential meetings and reprimands.
- Team meetings are appropriate for most team activities. Off-site members may join via conference call, but all others should attend in person.
- Phone calls are best used for one-on-one follow up. Phone conversations lack facial expressions and body language, which constitute a large percentage of communication. If the other party is nearby, walk to their station instead of calling.
- Emails are appropriate for sending out status reports and other written communications. Emails lack voice inflection and tone, and are subject to reader misinterpretation. Be very careful.
- Texting lacks too much for business use. Save it for personal use.

4

Triple Constraint

The Triple Constraint is a triangle, which of course has three sides. It is extremely difficult to change one side without affecting the others. One side is the project scope, a second side is the project schedule, and the third is project cost. There is also a fourth component—quality. Quality must never be compromised.

The project manager must ask the project sponsor, "When push comes to shove, which is most important: scope, schedule, or cost?"

I can almost guarantee the sponsor will reply, "All of these are important. You must meet expectations for all three."

Sometimes, many times, that is unrealistic. The scope may increase, resources may be pulled from the project, estimates may be wrong, and even budgets can change. There are many things that can affect scope, schedule and cost.

Explain to the sponsor what may affect the Triple Constraint. Then ask her to not only pick the most important one, but rank them (most important, next important, least important). Assure the sponsor every attempt will be made to hit the target on all three, but the project manager must know what can and cannot bend in a crisis.

My bet is the sponsor will then provide direction.

5

The Schedule

Ask many project leaders to show you their project plan and they'll immediate hand you their schedule. A plan and a schedule are different things. Project plans include several planning documents, as professional project managers know. The schedule is just one of those, but is the most frequently referenced document, as well as the one that changes most often.

The schedule is a diagram showing the tasks to be done, when each should start and end, and the relationship between tasks. A properly constructed schedule will allow for changes to ripple through the remaining schedule, changing the start date of any affected tasks. Use a project scheduling tool, such as "Microsoft Project," which is the most widely used project scheduler.

Creating an easily updateable schedule can be difficult for someone unfamiliar with the nuances of the tool. Training is recommended, and is offered by many computer training companies.

The project schedule is so important to so many people, some project managers distribute the schedule with the project status report. Should you choose to do this, make sure all recipients are authorized to view the schedule.

Below are step-by-step instructions for creating a schedule that can be modified as the project progresses.
1. With the project team, list the tasks necessary to complete the project.
2. Order and group the tasks by project phase. Indent the tasks within each phase.
3. Within each phase, order the tasks chronologically.
4. Establish dependencies between tasks. A task should be below any tasks it is dependent upon. Also determine which tasks can be done simultaneously.
5. Some tasks cannot start until a predetermined date. Update the start date of these, including the first task.
6. Assign a person to each task.
7. Enter an estimate for the duration of each task. The estimate should come from the assignee, and an end date agreed upon.
8. Enter any lengthy vacations affecting resource availability.
9. Optimize the plan by fine-tuning estimates.

Within the schedule, estimates will determine whether the project team becomes heroes or goats. Overestimate all tasks to allow for contingencies. Add 25% to the amount of time expected for each task. If you meet the schedule, you and your team will be heroes. *Beating the schedule is a huge win for everyone, and the team will* be superheroes. But come in late, and management and customers will be disappointed—the team will be goats.

Since estimates should come from the assigned person, let the team know you will be adding the contingency, not them. Contingency planning should only be done once, and by the project manager. The schedule should be aggressive and achievable.

It is imperative team members understand they will be held accountable for their estimates. They must meet the schedule. One week prior to each task start date, the project manager should notify the assignee. Issue an additional reminder the day before it is scheduled to start.

Track the progress of each open task. Minimally, the team should report to the project manager at each team meeting.

When an assignee cannot meet a scheduled end date, renegotiate a feasible end date with them. The project manager must determine how the change affects the entire schedule.

Whenever the project delivery date is impacted, regardless of the cause, revise the schedule immediately with the new end date. Then notify all stakeholders of the schedule change, and why. Be prepared to justify the changes.

Bad news should always be delivered as early as possible. Then maybe, something can be done about it. It is the project manager's duty to communicate news about the project, whether it be good or bad.

6

Execute the Plan

Throughout the project, the team will be executing the project plan. From the Kickoff Meeting to the celebratory luncheon, virtually every task performed by the team can be considered part of execution. This is where the project manager holds the team accountable for their assigned tasks, while he is busy managing and communicating.

Many reluctant-project-managers are worker bees as well. After all, you are good at what you do. It only makes sense you would be walking the walk, as well as talking the talk. Possibly, you might even be saving the most complex tasks for yourself. Who better to get things done the right way?

But have high expectations for all team members. In general, people rise to the level of expectation. On the flip side, if you doubt someone will perform well, they can sense that too, and are more likely to falter. Set the bar high. It's not a Limbo contest.

If you can foresee someone will not be able to complete a task, it is likely because of one of two reasons. Either the person lacks the time or the skill. If they lack the talent, then you have the *wrong person*, unless there is time and means to train them first. If they don't have sufficient time, then work with their resource manager to free them from other responsibilities. Help team members get what they want, and they will help you get what you want.

By definition, a project produces a product. Project execution is where the product is defined, designed, built, tested, and implemented. If your company has a product methodology, this is where it is used. Ask your manager and team members if the company has adopted any product development methodology.

Following are the five common phases of product development. Your methodology may have more phases, if these five are sub-divided.

The client is typically involved in all phases, except the Build Phase. An exception might be when client inspection is needed at checkpoints during the Build Phase. Without the client's participation in the project, there is little chance of creating the right product.

Define

Also known as scope, the requirements of the product are listed in the product definition. Only the requirements to be built during the duration of the project need to be defined.

Generally, the product developer interviews the client and documents the requirements. Though the product developer will attempt to document everything, there will be details that don't make it to paper. Hopefully, those details remain in the developer's mind, thus validating the reason why it was important for the developer to do the interviews.

The client should approve the written requirements. Once the product requirements have been approved, any further changes to the requirements must also be approved. But first the project team must determine how the changes might impact the schedule or cost. If it changes the delivery date or cost of the project, then the client and sponsor must agree *before* adding new requirements.

Scope creep is a high risk factor for project success, and must be dealt with professionally.

Design

Create a mockup or prototype of the product. The deliverables from this phase must be viewable by the client, who will approve construction.

Technical design may also be needed. These are documents prepared by developers, for developers.

Build

Create the product. This is much easier said than done, and is often the lengthiest phase of product development. Before proceeding, the project manager should review the design documents, then revisit the building estimates with the developers, who will be held accountable to meet the estimates. A revised schedule should be published for the project stakeholders.

The lead product developer must assure quality throughout development. This is typically done by inspecting each unit of work to make sure it satisfies the requirements and design. This is called unit testing, and reduces or even eliminates rework.

It is often tempting for developers to include additional features or functionality in the product. Don't do it. Resist temptation. The risk of failure increases with each new requirement. Got a new idea? Write it down, then suggest it to the client at a later date.

Test
    Testing is commonly divided into two parts. The lead developer tests what was built. Once the product is deemed complete by the lead developer, then the client performs their acceptance testing, and test results are given back to the lead developer.
    A test plan may be useful. If so, it is usually prepared by the developers, and it steps the client through the testing of the requirements and design.

Implement
    Perform the final steps to place the product in the hands of the client. Think hard about it. Depending on the product, these steps may be simple or complex.

7

Celebrate

The final task on the project schedule should be a team celebration. It is appropriate to budget and plan a celebratory lunch or dinner. The team deserves to be recognized and rewarded for a job well done. Also invite the sponsor and anyone who did *significant* work on the project.

There may be many people who made minor contributions to the project. They should not be included in the celebration. To involve them would only cheapen the reward for those who really did the bulk of the work.

At the celebration, the project manager should publically thank everyone, then ask the sponsor to provide a few words of encouragement. Warn the sponsor ahead of time! Also ask the sponsor to pay the check.

At a final team meeting (not the celebration), go around the table and invite each person to name just one thing the team did well, and another thing the team could have done better. Keep criticism constructive, and absolutely no names and no finger-pointing! The project manager should take notes of what is said. These become the lessons learned.

    With the team, rank the lessons learned, keeping only the top three good things and the top three things that could have been done better. These may be shared with other project managers, the sponsor, and archived for future reference.

8

Not-Too-Soft Skills

You are good at what you do; but how are your leadership skills? While these are often referred to as soft skills, a leader cannot be soft. As a project manager, you must be firm and respected, but never feared.

What is a company's greatest asset? Ask this question to most employees, and the responses will likely be things like money, customers, employees, buildings, technology, or products. While all these are crucial, any company's greatest assets are its leaders. It is imperative they are trained in leadership, and lead effectively.

All prior chapters addressed the "hard" skills, and dealt with project management techniques, sometimes referred to as project methodology. This chapter is about soft competencies, which are used to lead.

Both hard and soft skills are necessary for a successful project, but soft ones are more difficult to master. These are more art than science, and do not come naturally. There are few, if any, born leaders. They learn how.

Consider a popular phrase, "There is no I in team." This usually means the team takes the credit. But there is a "me" in team. See it? Each team member should adopt the following ten two-letter words, "If it is to be, it is up to *me*." The project manager should live by it, and instill a sense of project ownership in every team member.

Project Team Management

Treat team members like they will make difference, and they will. Solicit information and opinions from them. Listen, then make the best decision, and stand by it. Hold others accountable for their decisions and actions, and ask them to hold their subordinates equally accountable.

While it is good to get input from the team, it is not a democratic process. The project manager is responsible for project decisions, and must make those. You stand alone.

Do not micromanage, which can cause others to lose their zeal and sense of accountability. Only a project in *deep* trouble requires micromanagement.

If help is needed, ask early. Doing so is not a weakness, but rather a sign of maturity. Asking late is usually too late. Be specific about what you are asking for, clearly defining both the problem and a solution.

Keep team communications open, but confidential when appropriate. Let them know there are no dumb questions, and you will be discrete about what leaves team meetings.

Often times, teams seem to include difficult people, who should be dealt with one-on-one. Address disruptive behavior and let the offender know how it affects the project. If this doesn't work, then escalate the problem to their resource manager, whose responsibility it is to develop their employees. While the project manager is not responsible for another's bad behavior, he still must find a way for the project to succeed.

Being too soft is the number one reason for project manager failure. You must effectively lead the team and be able to make tough decisions for the project. Run the project like it is your business. Here are a few examples of a project manager who is too soft:
- Doesn't hold others accountable.
- Avoids conflict by delaying decisions or skirting issues.
- Tries to be a friend, but instead loses respect as a leader.
- Doesn't offer constructive criticism.
- Unwilling to defend the project plan to management or the client.
- Delays escalating unresolved issues.
- Accepts responsibility without authority.
- Accepts responsibility, but does not exercise authority.
- Doesn't follow standard project management practices.
- Poor inspection of work.
- Doesn't ask for help.
- Doesn't seek training for self or team.
- Doesn't delegate.

A project manager must be respected by the team and the sponsor. But respect is rarely automatic. It is obtained by your own actions. Below are behaviors that make someone worthy of respect:
- Appear calm and in control, even when you're not.
- Have high expectations for others and yourself.
- Look for solutions, not reasons to quit.
- Empower others to do their job.

- Develop good working relationships. Get to know what drives each team member.
- Maintain a positive outlook. Attitude is contagious.
- Be a role model for the team.
- Teach team members how to communicate.
- Make your boss and the project sponsor look good without brown-nosing.
- Count to ten. Draft sensitive emails, but hold those overnight before sending.
- Admit when you are wrong.
- Listen.

Show you are listening by making eye contact, restating what you heard, and by keeping your responses short. Be flexible, and accept new ideas.

Body language is a big part of showing you are listening. Face the speaker, and nod occasionally. Take notes. Do not fold your arms, as this indicates lack of interest. Above all, do not use your phone for any reason. Turn it off.

Issue Resolution

Throughout the project, issues will arise. These often threaten progress and must be addressed immediately. If not, the project may bog down or even fail. Depending on the severity of the issue, the project manager can decide when to address the issue. Some require same day attention, while others may wait until the next team meeting.

Any issue needs to be assigned to the responsible person. The project manager should discuss the issue with that person, and agree on how to resolve the issue and when it will be done. Then the project manager can publish the issue, along with the action plan and the expected resolution date. This can be done on the project status report.

Once an issue is resolved, let all the appropriate parties know, thanking the assignee. Closing out issues allows full energy to be spent on the tasks ahead.

If an issue is not resolved by the agreed date, then escalation may be necessary. After further discussion with the assignee, the project manager may involve others such as the assignee's resource manager or the project sponsor. The latter should only be involved for critical issues.

A final word

As in sports, if you play to not lose, you are more likely to lose. Play to win. Don't be afraid to make a mistake, or your chances are greater to do so. If a blunder is made, get up, shake it off, and move on.

If you are not making mistakes, you are not trying hard enough. Mistakes are stepping stones to success, if we will only learn from our missteps.

Lastly, use a leader's secrets—focus, boldness, and passion.

Author

Jeffrey Probst, PMP

Jeff enjoyed a long career as a software developer and a project manager. He is a strong believer in doing the right thing, and doing things right. Now retired, he loves traveling, hiking, fishing, and good food. He writes about his lifelong passions, and project management is one of those. He has also written books on money management, backpacking, High Uinta trail guides, and most recently, adventure/inspirational novels.